How to Look After Your Church

Published for the Council for the Care of Churches

CHURCH HOUSE PUBLISHING
Great Smith Street, London SW1P 3NZ

ISBN 0 7151 7561 0

Published for the Council for the Care of Churches
by Church House Publishing

First published 1970
Third edition 1991

© Central Board of Finance of the Church of England 1991

PREFACE

Some ten years have passed since the last revision of *How To Look After Your Church*. This new edition appears at an appropriate time, as the Care of Churches and Ecclesiastical Jurisdiction Measure has received the Royal Assent. Although the Measure may not have come into force when this edition appears, its provisions are included in the text.

The Council wishes to thank all those who were involved in the preparation of this new edition, especially Mr Donald Findlay, Mr Jonathan Goodchild, Mr David Harte, Mr Jonathan MacKechnie-Jarvis, Mr Ian Stewart RIBA and Mrs Nancy Wilkinson.

Mr Christopher Dalton provided all the photographs for the booklet, and we are very grateful to him.

Printed in England by Tasprint

CONTENTS

Parish churches are landmarks and focal points in the past history and present life of the community.

INTRODUCTION

England is remarkably fortunate in its inheritance of about 16,000 parish churches of many kinds, of many dates and styles, situated in town centres, villages and remote fields, which stand as silent witnesses to the Christian faith. Although together these churches form the largest stock of historic buildings in the country, the great strength of the Anglican system is that responsibility for their care and maintenance rests not at the centre but within each parish, with those who use the churches day by day and week by week. The incumbent, churchwardens and the parochial church council have clearly defined responsibilities in this area. Few of them, however, are likely to have particular professional knowledge of the care of a church building, its contents and churchyard, and so this booklet is intended to offer straightforward advice about the day-to-day care of a church. There is much in the way of regular observation and maintenance that can be carried out by parishioners without the expenditure of immense time and trouble during the years between the repairs recommended by the quinquennial inspection.

The principal enemy of all buildings, whether our churches or the houses in which we live, is moisture, which is the root cause of all types of rot and other forms of decay. The routine tasks advocated in this booklet, such as the provision of ventilation and the care and maintenance of gutters, downpipes and gulleys, can prevent at little or no expense the onset of decay which, if left to spread, may eventually cost enormous sums to rectify.

The Council for the Care of Churches publishes a range of more detailed booklets on the care of churches, mentioned in the relevant sections below. A list is to be found on page 31.

PAROCHIAL RESPONSIBILITY

The freehold of the church building is generally vested in the incumbent, and the furnishings and ornaments of the church are owned by the churchwardens. However, as a famous case in the courts explained, a parish church 'belongs not to any one generation, nor are its interests and condition the exclusive care of those who inhabit the parish at any one period of time'. For that reason, any alteration, repair or addition to the church or its furnishings can only be carried out under the authority of a faculty (see p.22 below).

The major responsibility for looking after a church lies with the parochial church council, which is entrusted with the care, maintenance and insurance of the building. In practice, however, PCCs often delegate this responsibility to a fabric committee or to one or two members of the PCC who can undertake routine maintenance, and ensure that the recommendations of the quinquennial inspection report are implemented (see below).

Good record-keeping is essential, and the churchwardens are required to maintain an inventory and a log book of all repairs, alterations and additions to the church. (See p.18 below).

Every year the churchwardens, in consultation with the incumbent, are required by the Care of Churches and Ecclesiastical Jurisdiction Measure to inspect (or arrange for an inspection of) the fabric of the church and all the furnishings and property. Guidance for this inspection is set out below. The churchwardens are also required to prepare an annual report on the fabric and furnishings of the church, giving details of the results of the annual inspection, and works of repair and maintenance carried out in the previous year. This report should be submitted to the meeting of the PCC before the annual parochial church meeting and thereafter, with any amendments which have been made by the PCC, to the annual parochial church meeting itself.

THE QUINQUENNIAL INSPECTION SYSTEM

The good state of repair of England's parish churches owes much to the Inspection of Churches Measure 1955, which established a system for the inspection of each church at least every five years by an approved architect. The inspection report is a comprehensive document, which sets out the items needing attention, from major matters such as the repair of towers or roofs, to the routine painting of wood and metal. The report's recommendations will be arranged in order of priority, usually *urgent, essential within the next 18 months, essential within the quinquennium* and *desirable*.

Once an inspection report has been received, the PCC and its fabric committee, if it has one, should examine the recommendations and discuss their implementation. If finance is available, the PCC should request the architect to draw up a specification and to seek tenders prior to the submission of an application for a faculty for the work.

Grants for major repairs may be available if the church is of particular historic or architectural interest. (See p.25 below.) If funds are insufficient, consideration may be given to phasing the work over a period of time. Parishes are strongly advised, however, to plan ahead for the likely cost of repairs arising from the quinquennial inspection, for example by placing an appropriate sum annually in a deposit account. Some items in the report, such as the clearance of gutters or attention to loose floorboards, could be tackled by a member of the congregation or a local builder straight away. If, however, it is intended to use experienced voluntary labour for more significant items in the report such as redecoration, the architect's advice should be sought and he/she should specify and monitor the work.

The architect will recommend that the electrical installation and any lightning conductor should be tested at the time of the quinquennial inspection by a competent person.

As was explained earlier, the Inspection of Churches Measure provided for the inspection of churches by an architect. The provision is amended by the Care of Churches and Ecclesiastical Jurisdiction Measure, and churches may now be inspected instead by members of the Royal Institution of Chartered Surveyors qualified as chartered building surveyors. The choice has to be confirmed by the Diocesan Advisory Committee for the Care of Churches (DAC), which will look carefully at an architect's or surveyor's qualifications and experience before agreeing to an appointment. For that reason an individual must be appointed rather than a firm of architects or surveyors. Advice is available from the DAC on the choice of an architect or surveyor.

Further details of the quinquennial inspection system are available in *A Guide to Church Inspection and Repair.*

ROUTINE MAINTENANCE

If the recommendations of the quinquennial inspection report are swiftly implemented, few problems should arise with the fabric of the church until the next inspection. However, various items of housekeeping will be required in order to keep the building in good order, in particular to keep the structure dry. To this end, it is an excellent policy for someone in the parish (perhaps a churchwarden or someone designated as fabric officer) to carry out a regular systematic examination of the building. An annual inspection is required by the Care of Churches and Ecclesiastical Jurisdiction Measure, but an inspection every six months would be admirable. Any defects, when noticed at an early stage, would cost far less to remedy than if they are left to worsen: a broken downpipe is far easier to remedy than an outbreak of dry rot.

Rainwater Disposal Systems

Gutters and downpipes help to keep a building in good condition by taking rainwater safely away. If the rainwater goods become blocked or broken, damage to the building can quickly occur, possibly leading to dry rot or death watch beetle. Gutters are easily blocked by leaves, moss and other rubbish, so it is vital that they are cleared *at least every six months*, preferably after the autumn leaves have fallen and in the early summer. Downpipes, gulleys, drainage channels and flat roofs should also be cleared. If access is difficult, an arrangement with a local builder can be a good solution. Snow should be cleared in winter.

Gutters become blocked easily, so they should be cleared at least every six months before damp begins to seep into the walls.

When examining the interior of a church, note any stains on plaster, which may indicate a fault in a roof or blocked gutter.

When examining the exterior of the building, look at the joints between each length of gutter or downpipe to see if the connection is sound. Stains on a wall, moss or weeds are all signs of a defect in a rainwater disposal system. It is a useful exercise to examine the system during heavy rain to see if any of the downpipes are damaged or the hopper heads blocked and overflowing.

Valley gutters are particular danger points and should be examined for cracks in their lead lining when gutters are cleared. Look also at the corresponding area inside the church to see that there are no stains or plaster blisters which would indicate that the gutter above is leaking.

Iron downpipes should be painted every five years, and the quinquennial inspection report should cover this item.

Leaks

Look for missing or slipped slates or tiles and for slits in metal roof coverings, and for corresponding stains in the interior of the church.

Walls should be kept free of ivy, and saplings growing close by should be cut down.

Walls

It is particularly necessary to keep the base of walls dry and free from vegetation. Ivy can do great damage to masonry and pointing and it should not be allowed to grow up walls. If there is already significant growth of ivy on walls, the main stem should be cut and treated with weedkiller. The ivy should then be left to die before being carefully removed from the wall. Small saplings can quickly grow into trees, so they should be cut down before their roots undermine the foundations.

Take note of any areas of pointing which need attention. Pointing in a stone wall must be executed with lime/sand mortar and not cement/sand mortar. This is definitely not a job to be given to a handyman, as great damage has been done to stone walls by the use of cement mortar which quickly cracks surrounding stonework. Professional advice is essential.

Windows

The iron bars which are part of the window structure require painting on a regular basis to inhibit rust, and again this item should be covered in the quinquennial inspection report. If vandalism is a problem, some form of protection for stained glass windows may be considered. Further information is available in *The Repair and Maintenance of Glass in Churches*. The CCC (83 London Wall, London EC2M 5NA) can also give names of firms experienced in glazing protection.

THE CHURCHYARD

An attractive and well-maintained churchyard is an enhancement to the building and a great benefit to parishioners and mourners, and all who use it. Obsessive tidiness is not required. *The Churchyards Handbook* recommends the simple expedient of cutting grass short beside paths and leaving the rest for occasional cutting. This keeps the proper character of the churchyard at nominal expense and encourages the growth of wild flowers and flowering grasses. Pathways can easily be kept clear of weeds with the careful and sparing use of weedkiller, perhaps on an annual basis.

The churchyard, like the church and its contents, is subject to the faculty jurisdiction. If it is proposed to fell a tree, the consent of the

An attractive churchyard does not require obsessive tidiness: many areas can be treated as a meadow habitat, and grass cut rarely.

local planning authority will also have to be obtained if the tree is subject to a preservation order or if the churchyard is in a conservation area.

THE TOWER

Exterior

From ground level, examine the parapets and the upper stages of the tower, if necessary with binoculars, looking for cracks, loose coping-stones, defective pointing or the growth of vegetation. Then, if practicable, ascend to the tower roof which is an excellent vantage point from which to examine the state of the church roofs and gutters. Note especially the state of valley gutters between roofs and of areas of flat roofing behind parapets. Look at the tower roof itself, especially in and near the gutters and flashings and the mounting of the flagstaff (which is particularly vulnerable to water penetration). Neglect of leaks here will lead to the damage of timbers below, including the bellframe. Repair of lead roofs is a skilled task, but as a temporary measure composition bandages can be applied to the affected area.

An efficient lightning conductor will protect the building by attracting a strike of lightning to the air terminal which is then carried down the conductor tape to the earth termination. However, the lightning conductor will be dangerous if damaged or not properly earthed. For this reason, the whole installation should be tested by a competent firm at the time of the quinquennial inspection. The down conductors should be examined regularly for signs of damage. If the church has a metal bellframe, this should have been bonded to the lightning conductor. Further information is contained in *The Protection of Churches Against Lightning*.

Note any unsafe ladders, floors, flagpoles, louvres and masonry and arrange for them to be repaired.

Interior

Birds should be kept out of the tower to avoid the build-up of debris which can encourage rot. Louvred openings can be made bird-resistant by placing plastic netting, stapled to a suitable timber frame, inside the openings. Once a tower has been made bird-proof, clean out all the debris and treat the timberwork with preservative.

A well-presented church is an attraction to visitors and potential members of the congregation.

Bells

If the church has a ring of bells, then one of the band should be appointed tower captain and deal with the maintenance required to the bells, reporting defects and providing an annual report for inclusion in the report on the fabric of the church. Guidance on maintenance is given in *Towers and Bells: a handbook,* published by the Central Council of Church Bell Ringers.

If the bellframe is wooden, watch out for woodworm attack and treat affected areas. If metal, it should be painted every seven to ten years. The quinquennial inspection should cover this item.

Clock

All turret clocks require regular lubrication, a routine job within the capabilities of a knowledgeable amateur. Useful information will be found in *Turret Clocks: Recommended Practice for Repair and Maintenance.* Most turret clock repairers will undertake this work on a contract basis, and annual servicing is recommended. The clock movement should be enclosed in a wooden case, made as dust-proof as possible and provided with electric lighting.

It is often difficult to find anyone who is prepared to undertake to wind a church clock regularly. An automatic winder can solve the problem, but it must be of sound design and correctly installed without damage or permanent alteration to the character of the clock. An automatically wound clock will still need routine maintenance and regular checking and resetting to time. Guidance is available in *Turret Clocks: Automatic Winders and Electric Drives.*

THE INTERIOR

A well-kept church is an attraction not only to regular churchgoers and passing visitors but also to potential members of the congregation, while a neglected and unloved church is unlikely to appeal to those who do – or who might in the future – attend it. If, however, it is clean, tidy and welcoming it will be able to play a vital role in the life of the parish. Bear in mind visitors who may be interested in it not only as a place of worship but also as a historic building; consider the production of a guide book if one is not already available.

The decoration of a church requires specialist advice.

Redecoration

If it is intended to redecorate the church, ask the inspecting architect to specify the work. Although it is normal practice to redecorate our houses with the modern emulsion paints on the market, these are not suitable for most churches, which generally lack damp-proof courses, the modern and effective method of avoiding damp. Although older walls are quite good at keeping moisture at bay, this efficiency relies on free evaporation from both the inside and outside surfaces. Paint does not allow moisture to travel freely, and it is therefore normal practice to use limewash in redecoration as this does not provide an impervious barrier. Further information can be found in *Redecorating Your Church*.

Electrical Installations

If any change is intended to the electrical system of the church (such as the installation of a new socket or a light) it should be carried out by a contractor registered with the National Inspection Council for

Electrical Installation Contracting, to the same high standards as would be specified for a rewiring of the whole church. Extension leads and other temporary devices should not be allowed. *Lighting and Wiring of Churches* gives advice on lighting schemes and the technical requirements for all electrical wiring in churches. Advice on sound systems is contained in *Sound Amplification in Churches*.

Heating and Ventilation

Central heating boilers need regular maintenance, most easily covered by an annual maintenance contract. The vicinity of the boiler should be kept free from combustible material.

Any proposed change to a heating system should be discussed with the parish's architect at an early stage as it can affect the furnishings in the church, particularly the organ.

Some parishes 'solve' their heating problems with portable flueless gas heaters, which are low in both capital and running costs. These heaters discharge significant amounts of water vapour into the air which can give rise to problems with the building. These heaters are not generally recommended therefore for use in churches except as a local top-up to background heat. Good ventilation is essential (see below). Portable heaters are also a special fire hazard and care should be taken that they are not left unattended and that nothing combustible or subject to damage from direct heat is left within their immediate vicinity. Advice on heating is contained in *Heating Your Church*.

Ventilation helps keep the building in good condition, particularly where dampness and condensation are experienced. Leaving the windows of the building open regularly on dry days so that the building can be well aired is much to be desired, as is the practice of leaving doors open in fine weather provided wire screens are fitted to keep out birds.

Church Plate

For many churches, the communion silver will be the most valuable small item owned by the parish and its proper care is therefore most important. Communion plate and valuable crosses and candlesticks should be kept in a locked safe, and insurance for a good modern replacement should be kept up to date. After use, the plate should be

Ventilation helps keep a church in good condition.

carefully washed, dried and stored in soft baize bags. Old plate is often fragile and should be polished gently, if necessary, with a clean chamois leather. Frequent polishing is neither desirable nor usually necessary. For more modern plate, proprietary cleaning materials are suitable. See *The Care of Church Plate*.

Floors and Floor Coverings

Apart from keeping the church clean and attractive, the regular sweeping of floors and vacuuming of carpets will keep the floor in good condition. A large doormat at the entrance to the church will limit the amount of abrasive grit which is brought into the building, and the mat should be removed and shaken regularly. Carpets with rubber backing should not be used as damage could be caused to the floor below by trapped moisture.

Organs

The organ is usually the most expensive item in a church, and it is certainly one of the most vulnerable to fire. Ensure that the regular checks of the wiring in the church include the testing of the electrical circuits of the organ. The electric action or blower of an organ may well predate the remainder of the wiring of the church by many years, and it is therefore desirable for the organ to be on a separate electrical circuit which can be turned off after use. Ensure that the area around the blower is left clear (to avoid over-heating) and that access for maintenance is not hindered. Tuning and general maintenance can be arranged by way of a regular contract with an organ builder.

The organ is most sensitive to changes in temperature and humidity, and the organ builder should therefore be consulted about any new proposals for the church's heating system.

If the parish is contemplating a major organ project, the publications *Church Organs* and *Repair or Replace?* give full advice, including guidance on the relative merits of pipe and electronic organs.

Glass

The treatment of stained and painted glass is a specialist undertaking; if conservation work is considered desirable, the parish's architect

A dry rot fruiting body

should be consulted in the first instance. He/she will be able to name suitable conservators, if necessary in consultation with the CCC.

Clear glass may be washed with a soft cloth and water. Some nineteenth- and twentieth-century stained glass may also be suitable for careful cleaning, providing the paint is stable; if there is any doubt about this, seek specialist advice. Ladders must be securely rested on the mullions of the window so they cannot slip onto the glass.

Further details are contained in *The Repair and Maintenance of Glass in Churches*.

Structural Woodwork

The decay of structural woodwork both from damp and insects is a common problem in churches. Leaking gutters and roofs lead to water penetration which softens the timber and sets the decay in train. Much can therefore be done to prevent decay by regular maintenance of roofs and rainwater goods and by good ventilation. The most common types of decay are summarized below:

Dry Rot. A fungus which can be identified by warping of the timber, surface collapse, grey stains on the wood, cracks across the grain, a web of threads or a furry white deposit. It can often be identified initially from a mushroom-like smell and in an advanced state will produce rust-coloured fruiting bodies. Dry rot needs expert treatment immediately.

Wet Rot is normally limited to areas into which water has penetrated directly, and can be identified by a darkening of the timber and a split along the grain.

Death Watch Beetle attacks wood which has already been softened by damp and fungal decay. Once established, it is difficult to eradicate and may spread to sound wood. Small deposits of bore dust from April to July are evidence of activity. Exit holes are about 3mm in diameter.

Woodworm (common furniture beetle) can be identified by exit holes about 1.5mm in diameter. It rarely results in structural failure, and small areas of infected wood can be treated with one of the proprietary products on the market. Examine the structural timberwork for evidence of the symptoms, with the aid of field glasses if necessary.

The parish's architect should always be consulted where deterioration and preservation of timberwork is concerned; often, much money has been unnecessarily spent on the unsupported advice of interested parties. Valuable ancient woodwork has also been discarded needlessly.

Wood Furnishings

Cleaning should be carried out with a clean, dry duster which should be regularly shaken out. Dusters should be washed after use and loose threads removed. Feather dusters are not suitable as the feathers tend to break and can scratch the woodwork. Polish need only be applied occasionally, perhaps once or twice a year. Care should be taken to protect wooden surfaces from water damage. Flower containers should be placed on a mat and watered with care.

The cleaning of painted wooden surfaces should only be carried out by a conservator.

Paintings

Wherever possible, paintings should not be hung in full sunlight or illuminated by powerful artificial light. They should be well-ventilated and should be kept away from sources of heat.

The surface even of an oil painting is very delicate and should not be dusted or touched. If the painting appears to need conservation treatment, advice should be sought from the DAC or the CCC.

RECORD KEEPING

Terrier and Inventory/Log Book

The churchwardens are required by the Care of Churches and Ecclesiastical Jurisdiction Measure to compile and maintain a terrier of all lands appertaining to the church and an inventory of all articles. They must also insert in a log book a full note of alterations, additions and repairs to the church, together with supporting documents. The standard forms of terrier, inventory and log book are published by the CCC and these must be used.

Good photographs should be taken of communion plate and other furnishings, including stained glass, showing clearly details such as marks and inscriptions.

19

These requirements may seem to be excessive and burdensome, but problems have often arisen from the lack of such information. For example, if new measured drawings have to be prepared by each architect, heating engineer or other contractor because such plans and drawings have not been preserved in the past, this will lead to unnecessary expenditure. The log book should either include documentation, or give the location of the document.

A good photographic record of all the furnishings in the church, including stained glass windows, is of the greatest assistance as a historical record and also to assist the police following a theft, or a conservator following damage. Adequate photographs can be taken by an amateur, and useful practical advice is contained in an article 'The Photography of Church Furnishings for Record and Security' in the 1990 edition of the CCC's annual journal *Churchscape*. Photographs should be kept with the inventory in the church safe.

The Care of Churches and Ecclesiastical Jurisdiction Measure requires the churchwardens to send a copy of the inventory 'to such person as the bishop of the diocese concerned may designate from time to time . . . . . as soon as practicable after it is compiled and shall notify that person of any alterations at such intervals as the bishop may direct from time to time'. Details of the name and address of the designated person may be obtained from the diocesan office. Copies of photographs should also be included with the inventory.

The Measure also requires the churchwardens to produce to the PCC, as soon as possible after the beginning of each year, the terrier, inventory and log book and other relevant records together with a signed statement that the contents are accurate.

The archdeacon is required under canon law to satisfy himself that the requirement to maintain the terrier and inventory is being complied with.

Parish Registers and Records

Register books of baptisms, confirmations, banns of marriage, marriages, burials and services must be stored in accordance with directions made by the bishop of the diocese under the Parochial Registers and Records Measure 1978. Records (such as PCC minutes, faculties and civil parish records) should also be stored in accordance with these directions.

Registers no longer in use and in which the last entry is 100 or more years old must be deposited in the diocesan records office, as must records of the same age. Some PCCs wish to retain their registers and records which are an important part of their heritage, but this can only be done with the authorization of the bishop, whose permission will only be given if the diocesan authorities are satisfied that the records will be kept in accordance with the strict rules for preservation in Schedule 2 to the Measure.

FIRE PROTECTION

Many fires in churches are started by vandals. Good security is therefore the starting point in fire protection. If the church is left open during the day, it is desirable for a parishioner to be present to supervise visitors and to prevent smoking. Fire extinguishers should be provided: a minimum of two, even in the smallest building. The extinguishers should be checked and serviced annually by the manufacturers. The church's insurance company and the fire prevention officer will be able to advise the PCC in more detail on fire protection, including the type of extinguisher to be used in each part of the building.

SECURITY

Statistics show that every year almost one in four churches is likely to suffer from theft, vandalism or arson. Every possible measure must therefore be taken to keep the building and its contents secure.

Church plate should be locked in the safe immediately after use, as should any valuable candlesticks. Portable items (such as chairs or paintings) should be locked in the vestry or discreetly secured in the church. Further information is available in *Church Security: A Simple Guide* and from the parish's architect.

Simple measures to make a church secure will deter many a petty thief. Should a theft occur, recovery is much more easily effected if good photographs have been taken of all the portable and valuable items in the church – see Record Keeping (p.18). Particular attention should be paid to key security. Keys to the church itself should not be hidden in the church or churchyard and keys to the vestry or safe should not be kept anywhere in the building.

The church's insurers or the local crime prevention officer will always be pleased to give advice on security, especially the suitability of various types of safe, the security of small items, and alarm systems.

THE ARCHITECT AND THE PARISH

Although there is no legal obligation upon the PCC to employ the parish's inspecting architect for the specification and oversight of any repair, it is good practice that he/she should supervise the work by preparing specifications, choosing the contractor, monitoring the work, checking the accounts and certifying payments. It is, however, unlikely that a faculty would be granted for major repairs unless the architect is involved. Repairs carried out solely by a builder without any architectural involvement are often ineffective and ill-informed and may in the long term prove uneconomic. Work in stone or lead is no longer generally required from the ordinary building tradesman, and consequently these have become specialist crafts for which an architect's specification and monitoring is needed.

It is also desirable that the inspecting architect should be employed by the parish to oversee any work on the heating or lighting installation. Continuity of supervision is one of the essentials for good maintenance of any building.

FACULTY JURISDICTION

As was mentioned earlier, churches, their furnishings and churchyards are subject to the authority of the consistory court of the diocese, and no major repair or alteration may be carried out, nor may an item of furnishing be removed or acquired without its consent, which is given by way of a faculty. The chancellor, the judge of the consistory court, receives advice on applications for faculties from the Diocesan Advisory Committee for the Care of Churches (DAC). This committee comprises archdeacons, parish priests, architects, experts on heating, bells, organs and so on, and examines applications for faculty permission in great detail. The expertise of members of the committee is extensive and their guidance is freely available to parishes. It is therefore wise to make contact with the DAC at an early stage in the formulation of proposals. The DAC may send a delegation to the church to discuss a scheme on site with representatives of the PCC and the parish's architect. This will ensure that any alterations or improvements to the scheme are presented to the parish at an early stage and will also shorten the process when the time comes to apply for a faculty. Procedure for applying for a faculty varies slightly from diocese to diocese; in case of doubt, guidance should be sought from the diocesan registrar. However, it is normal practice for approval of the DAC to be obtained before a faculty is applied for, and the DAC's report and recommendation can be attached to the faculty petition form.

If there is any doubt as to whether a faculty is required for certain work, guidance should be sought from the archdeacon or the diocesan registrar.

The usual persons to petition for a faculty are the incumbent and churchwardens. The petitioners will have to enclose a certified copy of a resolution of the PCC relating to the proposed work. The resolution should state the number of votes for and against the scheme, so a careful note should be taken at the meeting.

Once the chancellor receives the application, he first considers whether the work may legally be done, and that it is right that it should be done. His discretion is a judicial one: he must not exercise it on the basis of his own predilections, or of administrative convenience, but from proper evidence and the best available advice. He must see that all those who have an interest in the care of the church or churchyard (mainly the parishioners) have an opportunity of learning that a faculty is sought, and of opposing the granting of it, if they so desire: to this end a citation is issued giving notice of what is intended and posted inside and outside the church. Sometimes the chancellor directs that a citation should also be issued to a person or organisation with a special interest in the case.

If the petition is not opposed, and the DAC has recommended the proposals, the faculty can usually be issued without delay. If not, the chancellor must hear the case either in open court or by written representations and determine it judicially.

A fee is payable to the consistory court when an application is made for a faculty. In some areas this is paid centrally by the diocese and the charge shared between parishes by way of the quota. Guidance will be available from the diocesan registrar.

The Faculty Jurisdiction Measure established a system whereby routine repairs, redecoration or alterations to an existing heating system could be authorized by an 'Archdeacon's Certificate'. This procedure was removed by the Care of Churches and Ecclesiastical Jurisdiction Measure and replaced by a simple system whereby archdeacons are entitled to grant faculties in certain minor and unopposed cases.

Although churchyards are subject to the faculty jurisdiction, the incumbent has a general right to approve the erection of gravestones of an ordinary character in the churchyard. In some dioceses the chancellor issues an instrument of delegation (often known as the Diocesan Churchyard Regulations) defining the powers of the incumbent to approve memorials which conform to certain specifications. This procedure is designed to ease the passage of uncontroversial applications; it is not designed to enforce uniformity. An applicant has the right to apply for a faculty where a proposal differs from the parameters in the diocesan churchyard regulations.

SECULAR PLANNING CONTROL

Churches in use for worship are exempt from certain provisions of the town and country planning legislation. This has now been consolidated in the Town and Country Planning Act 1990 and a separate Planning (Listed Buildings and Conservation Areas) Act 1990. This exemption is continued because of the value of the church's own system of care and control and it is in everyone's best interests that the faculty jurisdiction should in every respect be conscientiously respected. Briefly, many churches are listed as being of special architectural or historic interest, or are in conservation areas or both. However, the provisions related to listed building consent and special restrictions on demolishing buildings in conservation areas do not apply except that consent is required for the total demolition of a church, unless carried out by the Church of England under a pastoral scheme.

However, 'development' in the meaning of the town and country planning legislation is not covered by the exemption, and planning permission (as well as faculty permission) is required for additions to churches, as well as for works which affect the external appearance of the building; this includes seemingly minor items such as protective glazing to a window or an oil storage tank. Individual proposals may, in some circumstances, benefit from the permitted development rights contained in the General Development Order 1988 although there is no major exemption for church buildings. The permitted development rights may attach, for instance, to walls, fences and other minor elements of development, but guidance from the local planning authority should be sought.

Churchyards, or individual tombstones, can be scheduled as ancient monuments under the Ancient Monuments and Archaeological Areas Act 1979. It is an offence to damage or demolish or alter such a monument without the consent of the Secretary of State.

Trees in churchyards may be protected either by a tree preservation order or by virtue of their standing in a conservation area. Notice boards in churchyards are covered by a third system of control in addition to the planning legislation and the faculty jurisdiction, namely the Town and Country Planning (Control of Advertisements) Regulations 1984. A new notice board over 1.2 square metres is likely to require permission.

Further details of the application of secular planning control are contained in *The Churchyards Handbook*.

SOURCES OF GRANT AID FOR FABRIC REPAIRS

(1) Public Funds

The Planning (Listed Buildings and Conservation Areas) Act 1990 enables local authorities at all levels to contribute by grant or loan towards the maintenance or repair of historic buildings in their area, including churches. Local authorities are often conscious of the importance of churches in the town or village scene, and the impact of the church building in its wider context is often taken into account in deciding whether or not to make a grant.

If the church stands in a conservation area, both it and the churchyard might be eligible for a *Town Scheme* grant (including funds from English Heritage); contact the local authority for details.

Grants from government funds are available for historic churches in use and are administered by the Historic Buildings and Monuments Commission for England (English Heritage), Fortress House, 23 Savile Row, London W1X 2HE. Application forms should be obtained through the archdeacon (who has to countersign the application).

An application to English Heritage for a grant should be considered on receiving the quinquennial inspection report. After receiving the complete documentation, English Heritage will, if the church is of outstanding importance, themselves send an architect to visit and inspect. Specifications of work should not be drawn up by the parish's architect until it is known what work English Heritage is willing to grant-aid. The grant-making procedure inevitably takes time and English Heritage never makes grants in respect of works already started without its approval; for this reason, applications should be made as soon as possible after a quinquennial inspection report has been received.

Where grants are offered, they do not normally amount to more than 40 per cent of eligible repair costs, but there is a careful assessment of a parish's financial capabilities (as with most grant-giving procedures) and less, or occasionally more, than 40 per cent may be offered according to circumstances.

Applications are invited from all denominations, but the church or chapel has to be judged 'outstanding' for its architectural or historic interest by English Heritage. It may already be a listed building but grants can be given for any building which meets the criteria.

Once a grant has been given, English Heritage requires the parish to seek approval for any future works of alteration, addition or modification. The purpose of this condition is to ensure that no irreversible action is taken which will harm the church's architectural or historic value.

In submitting an application, good photographs are essential.

(2) Diocesan Grants

Many dioceses make some provision in their budget for grants and interest-free or low-interest loans for the repair of churches in the diocese. A number also have savings schemes to which parishes may contribute and from whose funds they may borrow. Enquiries should be made to the diocesan office, which may also have information on possible local sources of help for repair schemes, and give advice on fund raising.

(3) Private Charitable Foundations and Trusts

There are various bodies which give grants for church repair schemes and details are given in a free leaflet 'Sources of Grant Aid', available from the CCC. For more comprehensive information, it is worth studying the following, which should be available in public libraries:

Directory of Grant-Making Trusts, published by the Charities Aid Foundation, 48 Pembury Road, Tonbridge, Kent TN9 2JD.

Directory of Public Sources of Grants for the Repair and Conservation of Historic Buildings, published by English Heritage, 23 Savile Row, London W1X 1AB.

For structural repairs to historic churches (of all denominations) the main private trust is the *Historic Churches Preservation Trust*, Fulham Palace, London SW6 6EA. This body also administers the *Incorporated Church Building Society* which makes modest loans for the building, extension and repair of Anglican churches.

(4) The conservation of historic furnishings and fittings

Applications for advice should be made to the Conservation Committee of the CCC. The Committee administers various block grants (principally from the Pilgrim Trust) and co-operates closely with English Heritage in the allocation of funds for the conservation of historic furnishings.

FABRIC CHECK LIST

The following list gives an indication of the time of year when certain items of routine maintenance should be undertaken.

At appropriate season depending on weather:	Check visually all gutters, downpipes, gulleys and roofs especially when rain is falling. Clear snow (using only wooden or plastic implements without sharp corners, to avoid damaging roof coverings).
Spring and early summer:	Make full inspection of church for annual meeting. Check inventory. Check bird-proofing in doorways, and in tower openings, especially belfry louvres. Sweep out tower. Destroy any vegetation growing up the walls or nearby. Check for signs of insect infestation in roof timbers. Check ventilation systems. Spring-clean the church. Arrange for gutters, downpipes, gulleys, roofs and ventilation holes to be cleared.
Summer:	Cut grass in churchyard. Cut ivy growth on trees. Inspect tower and other roofs, making sure leadwork is watertight and gutters clear. Have the heating installation serviced before the autumn.
Autumn:	Arrange for gutters, downpipes, gulleys and ventilation holes to be cleared. Inspect roofs with binoculars from ground level.

Annually:	Arrange for servicing of fire extinguishers.
Every five years:	Remember that quinquennial inspection is due and ensure that the lightning conductor and electrical system is tested at the same time.

FURTHER READING

Titles published by Church House Publishing on behalf of the Council for the Care of Churches

Church Log Book (loose-leaf format). Ring binder available
Church Organs
Church Roofing, by Keith Darby
Church Plate, by Robin Emmerson
Church Security: a Simple Guide, by Richard Brun
The Churchyards Handbook
A Guide to Church Inspection and Repair
Heating Your Church, by William Bordass
It Won't Happen to Us (Advice on insurance)
Lighting and Wiring of Churches
Redecorating Your Church, by Ian Bristow
The Repair and Maintenance of Glass in Churches, by Jill Kerr
Sound Amplification in Churches, by Jennifer Zarek
Terrier and Inventory (loose-leaf format). Ring Binder available
Writing a Church Guide, by David Dymond

Titles published by the Council for the Care of Churches and available only from 83 London Wall, London EC2M 5NA

Bats in Churches
The Care of Church Plate
Churches and Archaeology
Guidelines for the Care of Textiles
From Decay to Splendour: the Repair of Church Treasures
Loose Stones: Architectural and Sculptural Fragments in Churches
The Protection of Churches against Lightning
Repair or Replace? A guide for parishes considering the future of their organ
Turret Clocks: Automatic Winders and Electric Drives
Turret Clocks: Recommended Practice for Repair and Maintenance

Published by the Central Council of Church Bell Ringers, c/o Penmark House, Woodbridge Meadows, Guildford, Surrey GO1 1B2

Towers and Bells: a handbook